Twenty to

Felt Brooches

with Free Machine Stitching

Myra Hutton

Search Press

First published in Great Britain 2015

Search Press Limited
Wellwood, North Farm Road,
Tunbridge Wells, Kent TN2 3DR

Text copyright © Myra Hutton 2015

Photographs by Fiona Murray

Photographs and design copyright
© Search Press Ltd 2015

Print ISBN: 978-1-78221-196-9
EPUB ISBN: 978-1-78126-256-6
Mobi ISBN: 978-1-78126-257-3

Suppliers
If you have difficulty in obtaining any of the
materials and equipment mentioned in this book,
then please visit the Search Press website for
details of suppliers: www.searchpress.com

Printed in China

Dedication
In memory of my Dad,
my sister Katharine,
and not forgetting Seth.

Acknowledgements
With huge thanks to my husband Trevor,
who constantly supports and
encourages my creativity.

Publisher's Note
You are invited to visit the author's website:
www.myrahutton.co.uk

Contents

Introduction

I was lucky to grow up in a family of talented creatives, so it is no surprise that my passion for textiles began at an early age when I was introduced to my Mum's miniature hand-cranked machine, and I quickly found I could manipulate the fabric into the shapes I wanted. I perfected the skills I was taught and went on to study textile art and design at college. Through my studies I experimented and developed techniques as an art form.

Through continued experimentation and a search for ways to represent and capture the essence of the countryside, I developed my own style through richly embellished felt landscapes. I am continually developing and honing my work and this has led me more recently to work in an illustrative way, producing contemporary scenes and images. My brooches have developed through combining my illustrative work with my handmade blended felts as mini wearable works of art. Free machine stitching is an ideal way of exploring this illustrative way of working, and allows you to move your project in any direction, and create your own freehand design.

The brooches in this book have been designed so that you can use either handmade felts if you are already a felt maker, or manufactured felt – the choice is yours. The skill range is such that you can start with an easy design, with the opportunity for development as you become more confident with using the sewing machine as a drawing tool. Some brooches incorporate small pieces of additional fabric, such as organza or fine cotton, some use a few hand stitches and some have small beads sewn on, so there really is something for everyone, and each one will be unique. Have fun and be proud of what you create!

Techniques and materials

Drawing with a sewing machine

If you have never used your sewing machine as a drawing tool, get plenty of practice before you embark on any of the projects. Control of the machine is key, so the more you familiarise yourself with the technique by 'doodling', the more control you will have.

If you are less confident of sewing over pinned work, simply tack fabric in place while working. In order to follow the designs in this book, trace the template onto thin pattern or baking paper. This can then be stitched through, sewing along the lines, after which you can carefully tear it away. If you are an experienced machine embroiderer you may like to try sewing the designs completely freehand.

Preparing the machine

You can draw with any machine providing you can drop the feed dog (the teeth that carry the fabric through when sewing); refer to the user manual for your particular machine. Attach a darning or embroidery presser foot. Set the machine to straight stitch. The length of stitch you make will depend on how fast or slowly you guide the fabric.

The embroidery hoop

A very experienced machine embroiderer can work without a hoop when using fabrics with body, but until that level of skill is reached, you will need to place your work in an embroidery hoop. Manufactured felt tends to be thinner and can easily stretch out of shape. For each design in this book I suggest attaching the work to calico stretched in an embroidery hoop. This method will keep your work flat and give you more control. The excess calico is then cut away before backing the brooch.

To stretch the fabric in the embroidery hoop:
- loosen the screw on the outer hoop
- place the fabric on top of the outer hoop
- place the inner hoop on top of the fabric and push it down to sit inside the outer hoop
- clamp the hoop together, tighten the screw and stretch the fabric as taut as possible

Preparing to start

When you are ready to start drawing with your machine, you must remember to:

- drop the feed dog
- place the embroidery hoop on the machine flat side down
- lower the presser foot
- by hand, lower the needle into the fabric and pull the spool thread to the top
- sew slowly, keeping the work flat and guiding the needle along the lines without pushing or pulling

Fastening on and off

When starting or finishing any stitching in these projects, make two or three stitches on the same spot.

Troubleshooting

To avoid jumbled thread underneath:

- check that your fabric is taut in the hoop
- check that the presser foot lever is down
- adjust tension if necessary

To avoid breaking needles check:

- you are guiding the work, not pushing or pulling
- the work is flat against the machine table as you work
- you are not travelling too fast

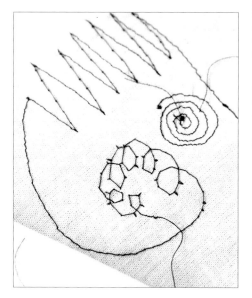

Materials

I make brooches from my own handmade felts for the top fabric; however, all the designs in the book can be made from manufactured felt. Manufactured felt is easily available from good craft shops. There are also a few fibre suppliers now offering hand-dyed, manufactured felt. These have more subtle colours, a textured finish and give a convincing handmade felt look. All designs require the main felt, strong backing felt, wadding/batting to give body, thread and a brooch back. Some designs require additional felts, several colours of thread, scraps of fabric, organza and a few seed beads.

Patterns

For most of the designs, you are required to trace and cut out the pattern to sew through. All the templates are reproduced in this book at half their actual size, so you will need to enlarge each one on a photocopier to 200 per cent before you begin tracing. You may need to make more than one tracing for some of the design stages. Leave the felt whole while working unless otherwise instructed – this will be cut to shape after the design is sewn.

Brooch backs

I tend to use brooch backs with a safety catch. To attach to the brooch, lay the finding (or brooch back) centrally on the reverse of the brooch. Use a strong thread, fasten on and sew with several stitches through each of the holes, taking care not to sew through to the front of the brooch. Fasten off securely.

Get plenty of practice at drawing with the sewing machine, as the more you 'doodle', the more control you will develop.

For information on stitches used in this book, please see **Stitching tips** on page 48.

Duck

Materials:

Tracing paper

Natural-coloured felt, 8 x 8cm
(3¼ x 3¼in)

Scraps of orange felt

Calico, 18 x 18cm (7 x 7in)

Wadding/batting, 8 x 8cm
(3¼ x 3¼in)

Backing felt, 18 x 18cm
(7 x 7in)

Black thread

Brooch back

Tools:

Embroidery hoop 16cm (6¼in)

Sewing machine

Paper scissors

Fabric scissors

Embroidery scissors

Pins

Needle

Tacking thread

Duck template: enlarge to 200%

Instructions:

1 Enlarge, trace and cut out the duck template, leaving a 1cm (½in) border.

2 Stretch the calico on the hoop. Lay the wadding/batting centrally on top of the calico.

3 Lay the natural-coloured felt on top of the wadding/battingand the paper pattern on top of the felt. Pin through all layers.

4 Cut the orange scraps slightly bigger than the beak and feet shapes. Lay these pieces in place under the pattern, tacking in place.

5 Sew the outline. Starting by the top of the beak, follow the outline around the head, sew down the curving line into the body and retrace to join the outline. Continue around the tail feathers and down to the right leg. Travel up to the top of the right leg, back down the leg and around to the lower point of the foot. Stitch up into the foot and back down. Continue around the foot up into the leg and back down to re-join the outline. Continue the outline sewing the left leg in a similar way, around the front and up to the neck. Continue around the beak, travelling across and back when you reach the top where it joins the body, finishing at the starting point.

6 Tear away the tracing paper pattern.

7 To make the eye, sew several stitches in a circular movement.

8 Carefully cut around the duck outline, leaving a small margin.

9 Trim away the excess wadding/batting and calico so that they sit just under the felt.

10 Place the work on the backing felt stretched in a hoop. Pin and stitch the outline. Start at the top of the beak and follow all the way around and back to the starting point.

11 Trim away any excess felt.

12 Sew a brooch back onto the centre of the backing felt.

Giraffe

Materials:

Tracing paper

Pale yellow or orange felt, 10 x 9cm (4 x 3½in)

Calico, 18 x 18cm (7 x 7in)

Wadding/batting, 10 x 9cm (4 x 3½in)

Backing felt, 18 x 18cm (7 x 7in)

Brown thread

Brooch back

Tools:

16cm (6¼in) embroidery hoop

Sewing machine

Paper scissors

Fabric scissors

Embroidery scissors

Pins

Needle

Instructions:

1 Enlarge, trace and cut out the giraffe template leaving a 1cm (½in) border.

2 Stretch the calico on the hoop. Lay the wadding/batting centrally on top of the calico.

3 Lay the pale yellow or orange felt on top of the wadding/batting and the paper pattern on top of the felt. Pin through all layers.

4 Sew the outline. Starting by the top of the muzzle, follow around the inside of the neck, around the body to the top of the tail. Follow the line into the tail, retrace up a few stitches and curve to the right, retrace to the centre and curve around to the left. Travel back up the tail to re-join the outline and continue around the bottom. Stitch across the top of the right back leg and retrace back to follow the leg down to the bottom; turn to sew across the bottom, turn to travel back up following the line across the hoof and back on the way. Continue around the remaining legs, sewing the hooves as before. Continue up the outside of the neck to the ear, up the ear, turning sharply at the point, down and across the head, back up into the right ear, down and back over the top of the head. Sew up into the left horn, make a circle at the top and travel back down. Repeat for the right horn. Continue across the top of the head to the starting point.

5 For the eyes, sew several stitches in a circular pattern.

6 Carefully tear away the tracing paper pattern.

7 Fill in the muzzle travelling backwards and forwards. Make spots randomly, by sewing an outline and filling in with a circular motion.

8 For the mane start at the top, follow the outer neck line stitching out to the left side and back at regular intervals.

9 Cut around the giraffe outline, leaving a small margin.

10 Trim away excess wadding/batting and calico so that they sit just under the felt.

11 Place the work on the backing felt stretched in a hoop. Pin and stitch the outline. Start at the top of the muzzle and follow all the way around, stitching over the tail, hooves and mane lines. Stitch over the horns to thicken them and back a few stitches over the head to give definition. Continue around to the starting point.

12 Trim away any excess felt.

13 Sew a brooch back onto the centre of the backing felt.

Giraffe template: enlarge to 200%

10

Teddy Bear

Materials:

Tracing paper

Pale brown felt, 9 x 7cm
(3½ x 2¾in)

Calico, 18 x 18cm (7 x 7in)

Wadding/batting, 9 x 7cm (3½
x 2¾in)

Backing felt, 18 x 18cm
(7 x 7in)

Dark brown and light
brown thread

Brooch back

Tools:

16cm (6¼in)
embroidery hoop

Sewing machine

Paper scissors

Fabric scissors

Embroidery scissors

Pins

Needle

Instructions:

1 Enlarge, trace and cut out the bear template leaving a 1cm (½in) border.

2 Stretch the calico on the hoop. Lay the wadding/batting centrally on top of the calico.

3 Lay the brown felt on top of the wadding/batting and the paper pattern on top of the felt. Pin through all layers.

4 With dark brown thread, sew the outline, moving the fabric in a jerky movement to create a 'furry' edge. Start at the top right shoulder and follow all the way around the head and back to the starting point. Continue from the shoulder around the arm and back up into the body, then travel back down to the right foot. Follow all the way around the foot and retrace to re-join at the lower body line. Continue around the left foot as before, up around the tummy and around the left arm, finishing at the top of the left shoulder.

5 Carefully tear away the tracing paper pattern and discard.

6 Change to light brown thread, keeping within the outlines of the head, and sew with a jerky movement, travelling across and back in zigzag lines to create the furry texture. Start at the top left, moving down with each row. Repeat for the body.

7 Change back to the dark brown thread. By eye, sew the tummy line across and back to thicken. For the eyes, sew several stitches in a circular movement. For the nose, make a triangular outline and fill. Sew a curve and back for the mouth. For the pads, sew double circular lines in position.

8 Carefully cut around the bear outline, leaving a narrow margin.

9 Trim away excess wadding/batting and calico so that they sit just under the felt.

10 Place the work on the backing felt stretched in a hoop. Pin and stitch the outline. Start at the top right shoulder, following around the head and body outlines as before and using the jagged 'furry' stitch all the way around and back to the starting point.

11 Trim away any excess felt.

12 Sew a brooch back onto the centre of the backing felt.

*Teddy bear template:
enlarge to 200%*

Butterfly

Materials:

Tracing paper

Pale blue felt, 9 x 9cm (3½ x 3½in)

Calico, 18 x 18cm (7 x 7in)

Wadding/batting, 9 x 9cm
(3½ x 3½in)

Cream organza, 9 x 9cm (3½ x 3½in)

Backing felt, 18 x 18cm (7 x 7in)

Dark blue, purple and pink thread

Brooch back

Tools:

16cm (6¼in)
embroidery hoop

Sewing machine

Paper scissors

Fabric scissors

Embroidery scissors

Pins

Needle

Instructions:

1 Enlarge, trace and cut out the butterfly template leaving a 1cm (½in) border.

2 Stretch the calico on the hoop. Lay the wadding/batting centrally on top of the calico.

3 Lay the pale blue felt on top of the wadding/batting and the organza on top of this. Pin and tack to the calico. Pin the paper pattern on top.

4 Using blue thread, start at the top right and stitch through the paper, following the outline around the wings to the bottom of the body. Travel up the body to the top of the wing, turn left across the top of the body and down to the bottom on the other side. Turn right at the bottom and back up to where you started the body. Turn the work and retrace the outline of the 'tail' to start the left wing. Follow the outline to the top of the body.

5 Follow the outline of the antennae and stitch down to the start of the inner outline. Follow the inner outline of the right wing, going around the base of the tail to the start of the left inner outline, and continue around the left wing.

6 Carefully tear away the tracing paper pattern.

7 Starting at the base of the left antenna, fill the shape using forwards and backwards stitches on the straight part and a circular movement at the top. Repeat for the right side, finishing at the base, then sew a few stitches to curve the top of the body. Sew down the body between the two lines, travelling with a zigzag motion.

8 Change to purple thread and use the zigzag method to travel between the outer and inner outlines of the wings.

9 Sewing by eye (or if preferred, make a second paper pattern to stitch through and lay in place), stitch the outline of the symmetrical teardrop markings on the bottom of the wings. Follow each line twice around to thicken them.

10 Change to pink thread. Make the markings inside the purple shapes using a filling stitch. Stitch the swirls at the top of the wings starting at the outside, then curling inwards and retracing to thicken them.

11 Carefully remove any paper if used.

12 Cut around the butterfly outline, leaving a narrow margin.

13 Trim away excess wadding/batting and calico so that they sit just under the felt.

*Butterfly template:
enlarge to 200%*

14 Place the work on the backing felt stretched in a hoop. Pin and stitch the outline. Start at the top of the right wing and follow around the whole outline, finishing at the starting point.

Travel down and up the body, and stitch around the inner outlines.

15 Trim away any excess felt and sew a brooch back onto the centre of the backing felt.

Cat

Materials:

Tracing paper

Natural-coloured felt, 8 x 9cm (3¼ x 3½in)

Scraps of coloured felt for necklace and flowers

Calico, 18 x 18cm (7 x 7in)

Wadding/batting, 8 x 9cm (3¼ x 3½in)

Backing felt, 18 x 18cm (7 x 7in)

Black, green and yellow thread

Brooch back

Tools:

16cm (6¼in) embroidery hoop

Sewing machine

Paper scissors

Fabric scissors

Embroidery scissors

Needle

Pins

Instructions:

1 Enlarge, trace and cut out the cat template leaving a 1cm (½in) border.

2 Stretch the calico on the hoop. Lay the wadding/batting centrally on top of the calico, the natural-coloured felt on top of the wadding/batting, and the paper pattern on top of the felt. Pin all layers in place.

3 Using black thread, starting at the right of the head and stitching through the paper, follow the outline for the head, returning to the starting point. Follow the chin line and back again in a jerky movement forward and back to make a 'furry' stitch. Continue to follow the outline of the body with a normal stitch. Sew the outline of the body, sewing around the right paw and up the right leg. Stitch back down the leg, around the paw and back up the centre line. Return down the centre line in a jerky movement forwards and backwards to make a 'furry' stitch. Continue normally around the left paw and up the left leg. Follow back down the left leg and around the rest of the body and tail, back to the starting point.

4 For the face detail, sew through the pattern, making the outline of the eyes. Thicken the line with an extra line of stitching. Through the pattern, sew the outline of the nose triangle, starting and finishing at the bottom. Continue down the mouth line and curve round to the left, then follow the line back and curve round to the right. Continue back along the curve and up into the nose. Sew the whiskers, starting at the inner point, following the lines out and back again.

5 Carefully tear away the tracing paper pattern. Fill in the nose triangle with straight stitches, moving backwards and forwards.

6 Change to green thread and sew the eyes using a circular movement.

7 For the necklace, cut a scrap of coloured felt about 3 x 0.5cm (1¼ x ¼in). Pin it in place below the head. Using black thread and a circular motion, create the beads. Starting at the right, make one circle and continue around to start the next circle. Continue to the end. Thicken the outline of the beads with extra stitches. Then trim away the excess felt.

8 For each flower, cut four tiny circles from coloured felt and pin them in place. Starting at the centre, sew out and around in a circular motion to make four petals.

Cat template: enlarge to 200%

Change to yellow thread and make a few tiny stitches in the centre of each flower.

9 Make the claws with a straight stitch, moving backwards and forwards.

10 Cut around the whole shape, leaving a margin. Trim away excess wadding/batting and calico so that they sit just under the felt.

11 Place the work on the backing felt stretched in a hoop. Pin and stitch the outline. Start at the top by the left of the flowers with a normal stitch, changing to the 'furry' stitch for the rest. Follow around the outline of the body, moving up and down the outside lines of the legs. Continue around to finish at the starting point.

12 Trim away any excess felt and sew a brooch back onto the centre of the back.

Cat on a Mat

Materials:

Tracing paper

Orange or tan felt, 9 x 6cm (3½ x 2¼in)

Natural-coloured felt for the mat, 12 x 7cm (4¾ x 2¾in)

Calico, 18 x 18cm (7 x 7in)

Wadding/batting, 12 x 8cm (4¾ x 3¼in)

Backing felt, 18 x 18cm (7 x 7in)

Black, tan and green thread

Brooch back

Tools:

16cm (6¼in) embroidery hoop

Sewing machine

Paper scissors

Fabric scissors

Embroidery scissors

Needle

Pins

Instructions:

1 Enlarge, trace and cut out the cat and mat templates as separate pieces, leaving a 1cm (½in) border around the mat and 5mm (¼in) around the cat.

2 Stretch the calico on the hoop. Lay the wadding/batting centrally on top of the calico.

3 Place the mat felt onto the wadding/batting, matching the lower edges, and pin in place.

4 Using black thread, start at the centre top and stitch through the paper; sew to the top right corner, follow the fringe outline to the bottom, turn the corner for the bottom line, turn the corner for the left side and sew the left fringing as before. Return to the starting point. Carefully tear away the mat tracing paper pattern.

5 Pin the cat shape into position on the orange/tan felt and cut it out. Lay the felt cat in position on the mat and protruding wadding/batting, and pin it in place. Carefully matching the shape, pin the paper cat on top of the felt cat.

6 Starting at the top of the head, stitch all the way around the head outline, sewing through the paper along the outline. Follow the lines, reversing where necessary to stitch around the ears.

7 Once back at the top, follow the line around the body, curling up around the tail. Start again at the bottom to the left of the tail, and follow

around the right paw. Travel up and back down the leg, around the left paw and back up to the base of the head.

8 Sewing through the pattern, make the outline of the eyes. Thicken the line with an extra stitch line. Now sew the outline of the nose triangle, starting and finishing at the bottom. Continue down the mouth line and curve round to the left, follow the line back and curve round to the right, then follow the curve back and up into the nose. Carefully tear away the tracing paper.

9 Fill in the nose triangle with straight stitches, moving backwards and forwards.

Cat and mat templates: enlarge to 200%

18

10 Trim away any excess felt from the cat.

11 Change to green thread and sew the eye centres with small circular stitches.

12 Change to tan thread. Using the design as a guide, make random 'stitch stripes' on the body working from top to bottom. Move the work to the right and left as you travel, to create a zigzag effect.

13 Trim away any excess felt from the cat where it sits on the mat.

14 Change to black thread. Make claws with a straight stitch, moving backwards and forwards.

15 Sew the whiskers, starting at the inner point and following the lines out and back.

16 Carefully cut around the whole shape leaving a margin. Trim away excess wadding/batting and calico so that they sit just under the felt.

17 Pin the work on to the backing felt stretched in a hoop. Stitch the outline of the mat with a straight stitch. Start at the top of the mat and follow the outline, going around the fringing to the bottom and back up to the top along the straight outline just inside the fringe. Travel back down the straight line to the bottom; turn the corner for the bottom line. Sew the left fringing as before and turn the corner to finish by the cat's head.

18 Starting at the top of the body, stitch around the original outline of the cat in a jerky movement, back and forth to make a 'furry' stitch, reversing where necessary and finishing at the starting point.

19 Trim away any excess felt and cut carefully around the fringing.

20 Sew a brooch back onto the centre of the backing felt.

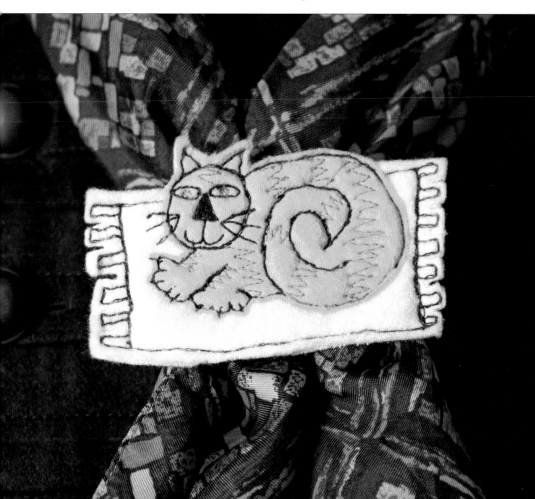

Dog on a Mat

Materials:

Tracing paper
Brown felt, 10 x 6cm (4 x 2¼in)
Natural-coloured felt, 10 x 6cm (4 x 2¼in)
Scraps of coloured felt
Very thin green ribbon, 30cm (11¾in) long
Calico, 18 x 18cm (7 x 7in)
Wadding/batting, 10 x 10cm (4 x 4in)
Backing felt, 18 x 18cm (7 x 7in)
Black, green and brown thread
Brooch back

Tools:

16cm (6¼in) embroidery hoop
Sewing machine
Paper scissors
Fabric scissors
Embroidery scissors
Pins
Needle

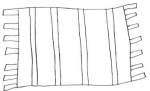

Dog and mat templates: enlarge to 200%

Instructions:

1 Enlarge, trace and cut out the dog and mat templates as separate pieces, leaving a 1cm (½in) border around the mat and 5mm (¼in) around the dog.

2 Stretch the calico on the hoop. Lay the wadding/batting centrally on top of the calico.

3 Place the mat felt onto the wadding/batting, matching the lower edges. Pin the mat pattern onto the coloured felt.

4 Starting at the centre top and stitching through the paper, sew to the top right corner, follow the fringe outline to the bottom, turn the corner for the bottom line, turn the corner and sew the left fringing as before. Return to the starting point, and carefully tear away the mat tracing paper pattern.

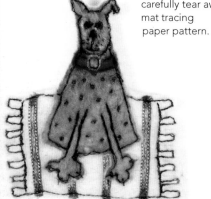

5 Cut the ribbon into pieces about 6cm (2¼in) long. Pin into position on the mat at regular intervals, about 1cm (½in) apart. Change to green thread. Change the machine setting to normal stitching, replace the presser foot and use in the normal way to sew the ribbon down close to each edge. Trim away excess ribbon. Trim away any excess mat felt at the top.

6 Change the machine back to freestyle, with black thread.

7 Pin the dog shape onto the brown felt and cut it out. Lay the felt dog in position on the mat and protruding wadding/batting, and pin in place. Carefully matching the shape, pin the paper dog on top of the felt dog.

8 Starting at the side of head and sewing through the paper, stitch all the way around the head outline. Follow the lines, reversing where necessary to give definition to the ears.

9 Once back to the starting point follow down to the body, stitch down to the bottom corner and turn, stitch across to the right leg, follow the line up the leg and back down, around the paw and up the left of the right leg. Follow back down the leg and across the base to the other leg, stitch as for the right leg. Follow the line to the corner, turn and stitch up to the head.

10 To sew the outline details of the face, start by sewing the outer circles of the eyes. For the nose, start at the bottom and make a triangle outline, finishing back at the bottom centre; then sew down and curve round to the left, follow the line back and curve round to the right, then follow the curve back and up into the nose.

11 Carefully tear away the paper. Trim away any excess dog felt. Fill in the eyes with circular stitches. Fill in the nose triangle with straight stitches, moving backwards and forwards. Stitch the whisker spots by hand with one small stitch each, fastening the thread at the back.

12 Change to brown thread. Sew random spots on the body with a circular motion, making small circles before filling in.

13 Make the claws with a straight stitch, moving backwards and forwards.

14 Cut and pin a colourful felt scrap for the collar, about 2cm x 0.5cm (¾ x ¼in), and stitch round the outline. Cut, pin and stitch a tiny circle from a felt scrap for the disc in the centre of the collar. Trim away any excess.

15 Carefully cut around the whole shape, leaving a margin. Trim away excess wadding/batting and calico so that they sit just under the felt.

16 Place the work on the backing felt, stretched in a hoop. Pin and stitch the mat outline. Start at the top of the mat, follow the outline around it, moving carefully around the fringe outline to the bottom and stitch back up to the top along the straight outline just inside the fringe. Travel back down the straight line to the bottom; turn the corner for the bottom line. Sew the left fringing as before and turn the corner to finish at the left of the dog.

17 Starting by the side of the dog's head, stitch the outline of the head, then follow around the outline of the body, travelling up and down the legs as before. Finish at the left of the head.

18 Trim away any excess felt and cut carefully around the fringing.

19 Sew a brooch back onto the centre of the backing felt.

Cocker Spaniel

Materials:

Tracing paper

Natural-coloured felt, 6 x 10cm
(2¼ x 4in)

Coloured felt for mat, 12 x 5cm
(4¾ x 2in)

Scraps of coloured felt for collar

Calico, 18 x 18cm (7 x 7in)

Wadding/batting, 13 x 7cm (5 x
2¾in)

Backing felt, 18 x 18cm (7 x 7in)

Black thread

Brooch back

Tools:

16cm (6¼in) embroidery hoop

Sewing machine

Paper scissors

Fabric scissors

Embroidery scissors

Pins

Needle

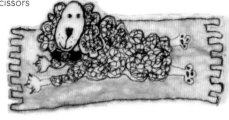

Instructions:

1 Enlarge, trace and cut out the dog and mat templates as separate pieces, leaving a 1cm (½in) border around the mat and 5mm (¼in) around the dog.

2 Stretch the calico on the hoop. Lay the wadding/batting centrally on top of the calico.

3 Place the mat felt onto the wadding/batting, matching the lower edges. Pin the mat pattern onto the coloured felt.

4 Starting in the middle at the top, stitch through the paper along the outline. Carefully tear away the mat tracing paper pattern.

5 Pin the dog shape onto the natural felt and cut it out. Lay the felt dog in position on the mat and protruding wadding/batting and pin in place. Matching the shape, pin the paper dog on top of the felt dog.

6 Starting to the right of the ear, stitch all the way around the dog's outline, sewing through the paper. Follow the lines, carefully reversing where necessary to give definition to outer curls, paws and so on.

7 Once back at the top, follow the lines of the head and ears again, reversing wherever it is necessary.

8 Stitching through the paper, sew the outer circles of the eyes. For the nose, start at the top

and make a triangle outline, then follow round until you are at the bottom centre; for the mouth, sew down and curve round to the left, follow the line back and curve round to the right, then follow the curve back and up to the nose.

9 Carefully tear away the tracing paper pattern. Fill in the eyes with circular stitches. Fill in the nose triangle with straight stitches, moving backwards and forwards. Stitch the whisker spots by hand with one small stitch each, fastening the thread at the back.

*Dog and mat
templates:
enlarge to 200%*

10 Starting on the body, make the curls by moving the work in a circular motion. Fill the body area and the top of the legs. Leave a small margin around the inner edge of the right ear. Thicken the line between ear and body with an extra line of stitching.

11 Make the claws with straight stitch, moving backwards and forwards. Make pads on the back paws with a circular motion, making small circles before filling in.

12 For the collar, cut and pin a colourful felt scrap about 1.5 x 0.5cm (½ x ¼in), and stitch the outline. Cut, pin and stitch a tiny circle of felt in a different colour for the disc in the centre of the collar. Trim away any excess.

13 Carefully cut around the whole shape, leaving a margin. Trim away excess wadding/batting and calico so that they sit just under the felt.

14 Place the work on the backing felt stretched in a hoop. Pin and stitch the outline. Start at the top of the mat and follow the outline around the mat, fringing and dog's head. Stitch over the head and ear lines to give more definition.

15 Trim away any excess felt and cut around the fringing.

16 Sew a brooch back onto the centre of the backing felt.

Cow Parsley

Materials:

Tracing paper

Natural-coloured felt, 10 x 10cm
(4 x 4in)

Calico, 18 x 18cm (7 x 7in)

Wadding/batting, 10 x 10cm
(4 x 4in)

Cream organza, 10 x 6cm (4 x 2¼in)

Backing felt, 18 x 18cm (7 x 7in)

Black thread

Brooch back

Tacking thread

Tools:

16cm (6¼in)
embroidery hoop

Sewing machine

Paper scissors

Fabric scissors

Embroidery scissors

Needle

Pins

Instructions:

1 Enlarge, trace and cut out the cow parsley
seed head template, leaving a 1cm (½in)
border. Trace and cut the organza outline
template with a small margin. Place the organza
pattern on the organza and cut the shape with
its margin intact.

2 Stretch the calico on the hoop. Lay the
wadding/batting centrally on top of the calico.

3 Lay the felt on top of the wadding/batting
and the tracing paper seed head pattern on top
of the felt. Slide the organza carefully into place
under the pattern, sitting it across the top of
the stem, pin the organza in place and slide the
paper off. Pin and tack through all fabric layers.
Place and pin the paper pattern back in place,
matching it to the organza shape.

4 Starting at the right and stitching through
the paper, follow the whole outline and back to
the starting point, catching the organza down
as you sew.

5 Sewing through the paper and working them
in pairs, stitch the stamen lines. Start with the
outer pair. Starting at the base, travel along the
line to the right side; at the top, retrace back
to the base and out to create the outer left
stamen line then back again to the base ready
to start the next pair. Create the other pairs of
stamens in the same way.

6 Carefully tear away the tracing paper pattern.

7 To create the 'fork' shape at the top of some
of the stamens, start with the centre pair and
stitch curving outwards to the right, follow
back and curve out to the left, and back to the
base; repeat with a slightly wider curved line
either side of the central pair. Repeat for the
remaining forked tops.

8 To make the daisy-shaped stamen, start at
the end of the line, curve out, around and back
to the base. Repeat four more times, finishing
in the centre. Repeat for the remaining daisy-
shaped tops.

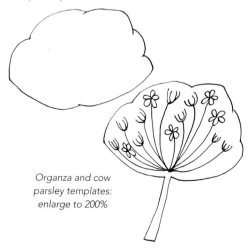

*Organza and cow
parsley templates:
enlarge to 200%*

9 Carefully cut around the whole seed pod, leaving a margin.

10 Trim away excess wadding/batting and calico so that they sit just under the felt.

11 Place the work on the backing felt stretched in a hoop. Pin and stitch the outline. Starting at the right side as before, follow around the whole outline.

12 Trim away any excess felt and organza.

13 Sew a brooch back onto the centre of the backing felt.

Baby Bird

Materials:

Tracing paper

Natural-coloured felt, 9 x 10cm
   (3½ x 4in)

Scraps of orange felt

Calico, 18 x 18cm (7 x 7in)

Wadding/batting, 9 x 10cm (3½ x 4in)

Backing felt, 18 x 18cm (7 x 7in)

Black, red and orange thread

Brooch back

Tools:

16cm (6¼in)
   embroidery hoop

Sewing machine

Paper scissors

Fabric scissors

Embroidery scissors

Pins

Needle

Instructions:

1 Enlarge, trace and cut out the baby bird template leaving a 1cm (½in) border.

2 Stretch the calico on the hoop. Lay the wadding/batting centrally on top of the calico.

3 Lay the natural-coloured felt on top of the wadding/batting and the paper pattern on top of the felt. Pin together at the bottom and centre through all layers.

4 Cut the orange scraps slightly bigger than the beak and crest shapes. Slide these pieces in place under the pattern, tacking in place. Pin all layers together at the top of the bird's body.

5 Using black thread and sewing through the paper pattern, start sewing the outline at the base of the crest. Follow the outline around the beak, sewing across and back along the line between body and beak. Continue along the outline to the bottom of the body, turn the corner to sew across the top of the legs and return to travel around the outline of the right leg and foot, across to the top of the left leg and all the way around the left leg. Continue along the outline, turning to travel around the tail and back up to the starting point. Follow the curved lines of the crest.

6 Carefully tear away the tracing paper pattern.

7 For the eye, sew an outer circle first and then in the centre, sew several stitches, using a circular movement.

8 Sew random circles for the spots on the body.

9 Fill the legs with straight movements forwards and backwards, and a circular movement for the knees.

10 Cut around the baby bird outline, leaving a narrow margin.

11 Trim away excess wadding/batting and calico so that they sit just under the felt.

12 Place the work on the backing felt stretched in a hoop. Pin and stitch the outline. Start at the base of the crest, follow around and across the top of the beak. Continue to follow the outline with a 'sketchy' stitch, moving backwards and forwards as you follow the outline, changing to normal stitch around the legs and crest, finishing at the starting point.

13 Change to orange thread. Starting just above halfway down the back and about 2mm (¹/₁₆in) in from the black outline, sew a line for the tail down and curling round into the curl of the tail at the bottom. Sew back up the line to the beginning to thicken it.

*Baby bird
template:
enlarge to 200%*

26

14 Change to red thread. Starting halfway down the back and about 5mm (¼in) in from the black outline, sew a second line following the shape of the orange line. Sew back up the line to the beginning to thicken it.

15 Trim away any excess felt.

16 Sew a brooch back onto the centre of the backing felt.

Owl

Materials:

Tracing paper

Brown felt, 8 x 8cm (3¼ x 3¼in)

Scraps of orange and yellow felt

Scrap of vintage cotton fabric

Calico, 18 x 18cm (7 x 7in)

Wadding/batting, 8 x 8cm
  (3¼ x 3¼in)

Backing felt, 18 x 18cm (7 x 7in)

Black thread

Brooch back

Tools:

16cm (6¼in)
  embroidery
  hoop

Sewing machine

Paper scissors

Fabric scissors

Embroidery scissors

Pins

Needle

*Owl and apron
templates:
enlarge to 200%*

Instructions:

1 Enlarge, trace and cut out the owl template leaving a 1cm (½in) border. Enlarge, trace and cut out the apron template separately.

2 Stretch the calico on the hoop. Lay the wadding/batting centrally on top of the calico.

3 Lay the brown felt on top of the wadding/batting and the paper pattern on top of the felt. Pin through all layers.

4 Using black thread and sewing through the paper pattern, sew the outline, starting at the top of the right wing and following it down to the bottom. Follow around the edge of the feathers and up the inside of the wing, return down and continue to the top of the foot, follow around the foot and turn right to sew across the top of the foot. Turn and sew to the top of the left foot, sew around and across as before, returning to the top left of the foot. Continue up the body to the top inside of the left wing. Follow back down the wing and around the feathers. Turn sharply and follow up to the left ear. Travel around the ear and across the head to the right ear. Follow around the right ear and back to the starting point.

5 Next, sew the wing feathers through the paper pattern.

6 Carefully tear away the paper pattern.

7 Using the apron pattern, cut from a scrap of vintage fabric. Lay the apron fabric in place across the owl's tummy. Sew the apron down while sewing across the lower body in rows of 'u' shapes. Starting with the top row at the left, sew down, curve around and back up to start the next 'u', finishing at the right. Make two more rows in the same way.

8 Cut two small circles for the eyes from the yellow felt scraps. Sew them in place around the edge of the circle. Sew the eyelid line as a curve from left to right, and return along the line, stopping at intervals to sew down and back up for each eyelash.

9 Cut a small triangle from the orange felt scrap for the beak. Lay in position and sew around the outline.

10 Carefully cut around the owl outline, leaving a margin.

11 Trim away excess wadding/batting and calico so that they sit just under the felt.

12 Place the work on the backing felt stretched in a hoop. Pin and stitch the outline. Starting at the top of the right wing, follow around the outline as before, turning sharply at the corners. When you reach the top of the head, sew back across the left ear slightly and continue across a little way into the right ear, finishing at the starting point.

13 Trim away any excess felt.

14 Sew a brooch back onto the centre of the backing felt.

Chicken

Materials:

Tracing paper

Orange or light brown felt, 9 x 6cm (3½ x 2¼in)

Scraps of red and yellow felt

Scrap of red organza

Calico, 18 x 18cm (7 x 7in)

Wadding/batting, 9 x 6cm (3½ x 2¼in)

Backing felt, 18 x 18cm (7 x 7in)

Black thread

Brooch back

Tools:

16cm (6¼in) embroidery hoop

Sewing machine

Paper scissors

Fabric scissors

Embroidery scissors

Pins

Needle

Instructions:

1 Enlarge, trace and cut out the chicken template leaving a 1cm (½in) border. Trace and cut out the wing separately.

2 Stretch the calico on the hoop. Lay the wadding/batting centrally on top of the calico.

3 Lay the orange or light brown felt on top of the wadding/batting and the paper pattern on top of the felt. Pin across the centre through all layers.

4 Cut the red felt slightly bigger than the comb and the wattles, carefully slide these pieces in place under the pattern, tacking in place. Repeat with the yellow felt for the beak and legs. Pin all layers together around edges.

5 Using black thread and sewing through the pattern, start the outline at the top of the head, following the line over the curve of the head, then up and around the comb, along the line back over the curve of the head and body, and around the tail feathers. Continue along the outline to the right leg. Follow the outline of the right leg and foot, and stitch across the top of the leg before continuing along the outline under the body. Follow around the left leg as before and continue up to the beak. Sew around the wattles and across the top of the beak. Turn and travel down to the tip of the beak, then turn again for the underside of the beak. Follow the jagged feather line between the head and body.

6 Sew the inner tail feathers through the pattern in the same way as the head feathers.

7 Carefully tear away the tracing paper pattern.

8 Using the wing pattern, cut from a scrap of organza. Pin the wing in place and sew around the outline, creating feather shapes at the end.

9 Sew a few circular spots on the chicken's breast as shown.

10 For the eye, sew several stitches using a circular movement.

11 Carefully cut around the chicken outline, leaving a narrow margin.

12 Trim away excess wadding/batting and calico so that they sit just under the felt.

13 Place the work on the backing felt stretched in a hoop. Pin and stitch the outline. Start at the top of the head and follow all the way around the outline as before, turning sharply at corners, finishing at the starting point.

14 Trim away any excess felt.

15 Sew a brooch back onto the centre of the backing felt.

Chicken and wing templates: enlarge to 200%

Swirly Bird

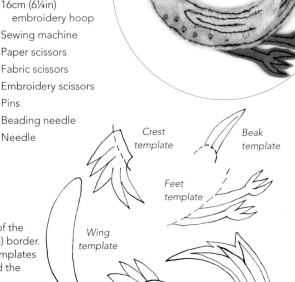

Materials:

Tracing paper

Pale blue felt, 10 x 10cm (4 x 4in)

Scraps of pink, yellow and white felt

Cream organza, 9 x 3cm (3½ x 1¼in)

Pale blue tulle, 9 x 6cm (3½ x 2¼in)

Calico, 18 x 18cm (7 x 7in)

Wadding/batting, 10 x 10cm (4 x 4in)

Grey backing felt, 18 x 18cm (7 x 7in)

A few seed beads

Black thread

Brooch back

Tools:

16cm (6¼in)
   embroidery hoop

Sewing machine

Paper scissors

Fabric scissors

Embroidery scissors

Pins

Beading needle

Needle

Instructions:

1 Enlarge, trace and cut out the body of the swirly bird template leaving a 5mm (¼in) border. Trace and cut out the crest and beak templates separately with a 5mm (¼in) border, and the wing with no border.

2 Stretch the calico on the hoop. Lay the wadding/batting centrally on top of the calico.

3 Cut the body shape from the blue felt and lay on top of the wadding/batting. Lay the paper pattern on top of the felt. Pin across the centre through all layers.

4 Cut the beak shape from the yellow felt and carefully slide into position under the head, tacking in place to the calico and wadding/batting, but not the bird head. Repeat with the pink felt for the crest. Carefully pull the bird head out of the way while you sew the outlines of the beak and crest. Place the crest pattern on top of the pink felt and pin. Using black thread and sewing through the pattern, sew the outline of the crest starting at the bottom left in the border, and following up and down the lines to create the plumes. Finish at the bottom right in the border. Place the beak pattern on top of the yellow felt and pin. Using black thread and sewing through the pattern, sew the outline of the beak, starting in the border at the top right, following down to the tip of the beak and back up, sewing into the border.

Crest template

Beak template

Feet template

Wing template

Enlarge all templates to 200%

Turn slightly, sew across to the top centre of the beak and sew down the centre line of the beak and back again. Finish at the centre top.

5 Carefully tear away the tracing paper pattern from the crest and beak. Lay the bird's head back in place with the body pattern on top and pin.

6 Sew the body outline through the paper pattern. Start at the top of the head to the left of the crest, following around the head and sewing the crest into place. Follow the curve, stitch over the beak to sew it into place and curve it up slightly to define the head. Retrace back to the outline and continue to follow the curve of the body into the tail. Turn the corner and sew along the tail feathers, turning sharply at each point. Continue around the body curve until you reach the starting point.

7 Sew along the inner tail feather lines, retracing to continue where necessary.

8 Sew a few circular spots randomly along the bird's back.

9 Carefully tear away the tracing paper pattern.

10 Cut a small circle from the white felt and place in position for the eye, sewing around the outline twice. For the centre of the eye, sew several stitches in a circular movement.

11 Using the wing pattern, cut one piece from the organza and two pieces from the tulle.

12 Lay the organza wing in place with the two tulle wings on top. Pin the wings in place and sew around the outline and centre lines twice to thicken, leaving the end of the wings free.

13 Sew the seed beads onto the tail feathers.

14 Carefully cut around the whole bird outline, leaving a narrow margin.

15 Trim away excess wadding/batting and calico so that they sit just under the felt.

16 Place the work on backing felt stretched in a hoop. Pin the head and tail. With a pencil draw legs on the backing felt in position. Unpin the bird and stitch the outline of the legs, making sharp turns for the claws, continuing the lines of the legs into the body backing by 2cm (¾in).

17 Place the body back onto the backing felt with the legs in the correct position. Pin in place. Check the fabric is still taut. Stitch the outline, starting around the crest, taking it as close to the body as possible. Repeat for the beak. Sew all the way around the main body starting at the top of the head, working around the head, body and tail as before and finishing at the starting point.

18 Trim away excess felt and backing fabric.

19 Sew a brooch back onto the centre of the backing felt.

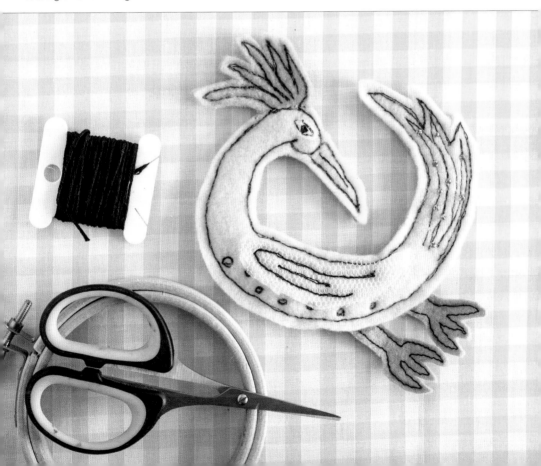

Poppy

Materials:

Tracing paper

Pink felt, 12 x 12cm (4¾ x 4¾in)

Scraps of green felt

Calico, 18 x 18cm (7 x 7in)

Wadding/batting, 12 x 12cm
   (4¾ x 4¾in)

Backing felt, 18 x 18cm (7 x 7in)

Black thread

Brooch back

Tools:

16cm (6¼in) embroidery hoop

Sewing machine

Paper scissors

Fabric scissors

Embroidery scissors

Pins

Needle

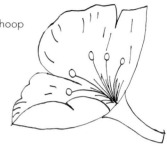

Poppy template: enlarge to 200%

Instructions:

1 Enlarge, trace and cut out the whole poppy template leaving a 1cm (½in) border. Trace and cut out the stem shape separately leaving a 5mm (¼in) border.

2 Stretch the calico on the hoop. Lay the wadding/batting centrally on top of the calico.

3 Lay the pink felt on top of the wadding/ batting and the paper pattern on top of the felt. Pin across the top and centre through all layers.

4 Cut the stem shape from the green felt, and carefully slide this piece into position under the pattern, tacking in place. Pin all layers together around the edges.

5 Using black thread and sewing through the pattern, sew the outline of the stem. Start at the top left of the stem, sew across the top, turn sharply to travel down to the bottom of the stem, across the bottom and up the left side to the starting point. Carefully peel back the pattern and trim away the excess green felt to just above the stitching, where it overlaps the flower part. Replace the pattern.

6 To sew the flower outline, turn the work upside down with the stem at the top. Start at the top right and follow down to the point at the bottom, turn sharply and follow the outer curve round and down into the flower, retrace the stiches to the top of the second curve, and follow the shape all the way around, dipping in and out of the far left petal and turning sharply to travel back to the top. Once back at the

starting point, swing into the flower and follow the line to the top, reversing and back to give shape midway.

7 Turn the work the right way up. Sew the stamens by starting at the bottom and following the lines of the stamens out and back to the base. Finish at the starting point.

8 Make the short petal markings twice to thicken the lines.

9 Carefully tear away the tracing paper pattern.

10 For the stamen tips, sew several stitches in a circular movement at the end of each stamen line. For the centre shading, start at the base and sew out and back in a fan shape.

11 Carefully cut around the poppy outline leaving a margin.

12 Trim away excess wadding/batting and calico so that they sit just under the felt.

13 Place the work on the backing felt stretched in a hoop. Pin and stitch the outline, starting at the top of the stem and following all the way around the outline as before, then onto the outline of the flower and back up along the left petal outline, finishing at the top.

14 Trim away any excess felt.

15 Sew a brooch back onto the centre of the backing felt.

Lily

Materials:

Tracing paper

Pale yellow felt, 12 x 12cm
(4¾ x 4¾in)

Scraps of green felt

Calico, 18 x 18cm (7 x 7in)

Wadding/batting, 12 x 12cm
(4¾ x 4¾in)

Backing felt, 18 x 18cm (7 x 7in)

Black thread

A few seed beads and
matching thread

Brooch back

Tools:

16cm (6¼in)
embroidery hoop

Sewing machine

Paper scissors

Fabric scissors

Embroidery scissors

Pins

Beading needle

Needle

*Lily template:
enlarge to 200%*

Instructions:

1 Enlarge, trace and cut out the whole lily template leaving a 1cm (½in) border. Trace and cut out the stem template leaving a 5mm (¼in) border.

2 Stretch the calico on the hoop. Lay the wadding/batting centrally on top of the calico.

3 Lay the yellow felt on top of the wadding/batting and the paper pattern on top of the felt. Pin across the top and centre through all layers.

4 Cut the stem shape from the green felt, and slide this piece in place under the pattern, tacking it in place. Pin all layers together around edges.

5 Using black thread, sew the outline of the stem through the paper pattern. Start at the top left of the stem, sew across the top, turn sharply to travel down to the bottom of the stem, across the bottom and up the left side to the starting point. Carefully peel back the pattern and trim away the excess green felt to just above the stitching, where it overlaps the flower part. Replace the pattern.

6 To sew the flower outline, turn the work upside down with the stem at the top. Start at the top right and follow along the lines, curving around to the point. Turn sharply and follow the curve, stopping to sew out to the left and back at the first petal marking. Continue to the point, turn sharply and curve around to the next point,

continuing around the outline, making the two petal markings as before and down a couple of stitches into the flower; retrace back to the outline and continue down to the next point. Turn and follow the curves, stitching back into the flower to create the right petal, retrace back to the outline, follow the curve, turn sharply at the bottom and follow the curve all the way around, finishing at the starting point. Continue sewing around, this time following the line of the petal at the front all the way around until you reach the outer line.

7 Turn the work the right way up. Sew the stamens, starting at the bottom and following the lines of the stamens out and back to the base. Finish at the starting point.

8 Make the short petal marks twice to thicken the lines.

9 Carefully tear away the tracing paper pattern.

10 Sew several stitches in a circular movement at the end of each stamen line. For the centre shading, start at the base and sew out and back in a fan shape.

11 Scatter a few beads onto the flower and by hand, sew them where they fall, fastening off at the back.

12 Carefully cut around the lily outline leaving a margin.

13 Trim away excess wadding/batting and calico so that they sit just under the felt.

14 Place the work on the backing felt stretched in a hoop. Pin and stitch the outline. Start at the top of the stem and follow all the way around the outline as before, then onto the outline of the flower and back up and around the front petal, finishing at the outer line.

15 Trim away any excess felt.

16 Sew a brooch back onto the centre of the backing felt.

Bouquet

Materials:

Tracing paper

Green felt, 12 x 8cm (4¾ x 3¼in)

Pink felt, 7 x 6cm (2¾ x 2¼in)

Scraps of white and pink felt

Calico, 18 x 18cm (7 x 7in)

Wadding/batting, 12 x 8cm
(4¾ x 3¼in)

Backing felt, 18 x 18cm (7 x 7in)

Dark green, light green, pink,
yellow and black thread

Brooch back

Tools:

16cm (6¼in)
embroidery hoop

Sewing machine

Paper scissors

Fabric scissors

Embroidery scissors

Pins

Needle

*Bouquet and bow
templates:
enlarge to 200%*

Instructions:

1 Enlarge, trace and cut out the whole bouquet template minus the bow, leaving a 1cm (½in) border. Enlarge, trace and cut out the bow template leaving a 5mm (¼in) border.

2 Lay the wadding/batting centrally on top of the calico. Lay the green felt on top of the wadding/batting and the bouquet pattern on top of the felt. Pin through all layers.

3 Using dark green thread, sew all the way around the outline of the bouquet, starting and finishing where the bow will sit. Carefully tear away the paper pattern.

4 Sew the flower stems with light green thread. Start in the centre under where the bow will be, sewing down towards the bottom and back to the centre; then move slightly to one side and sew another stem in the same way. Continue until you have a few stems evenly spaced out in the 'stalk' area, finishing at the starting point. From here, sew up into the flower area and back as before, but this time in a fan shape.

5 With dark green thread, make a few stems as before in the spaces between the lighter green stems. Make leaves as shown in the design. To make a leaf, start at the bottom point, working out and up to the top point then out and back to the bottom point, stitching up into the leaf and reversing where necessary to make veins.

6 Change to black thread. Cut small oval shapes from scraps of pink felt for the tulips and tack in place. To sew a tulip, start at the top left, travel down curving around the base and back up to curve around the top and swirl into the flower. Trim away any excess pink felt.

7 Cut circles from the white felt scraps for the daisies, about 1cm (½in) in diameter, and tack in place. Start sewing in the centre, swinging out slightly and back towards the edge, then turn sharply and swing in the same way back to the centre; repeat four times so you have five petals in total. Change to yellow thread and make the centre from a few stitches sewn in a circular movement.

8 Change to pink thread for the swirls. Start at the top and sew in a circular motion, travelling down as you go.

9 Trim away the excess green felt from the area where the bow will sit.

10 Carefully cut around the whole bouquet shape leaving a narrow margin.

11 Trim away excess wadding/batting and calico so that they sit just under the felt.

12 Place the work on the backing felt stretched in a hoop. Pin and stitch the outline. Using dark green thread, start at the top left of the floral part following the shape, stopping at the top of the bow on the right. Sew the bottom outline of the stems between the bow tails. Change to black and sew the very outer line of the bow.

13 Trim away any excess felt.

14 Sew a brooch back onto the centre of the backing felt.

Flowerpot

Materials:

Tracing paper

Green felt, 12 x 10cm (4¾ x 4in)

Brown felt, 7 x 8cm (2¾ x 3¼in)

Scraps of white, pink, magenta and yellow felt

Calico, 18 x 18cm (7 x 7in)

Wadding/batting, 12 x 14cm (4¾ x 5½in)

Backing felt, 18 x 18cm (7 x 7in)

Dark green, light green, brown, pink and black thread

Brooch back

Tools:

16cm (6¼in) embroidery hoop

Sewing machine

Paper scissors

Fabric scissors

Embroidery scissors

Pins

Needle

Instructions:

1 Enlarge, trace and cut out the greenery shape template, leaving a 1cm (½in) border. Trace and cut out the flowerpot template separately leaving a 5mm (¼in) border at the top and a 1cm (½in) border around the sides and bottom.

2 Stretch the calico on the hoop. Lay the wadding/batting centrally on top of the calico.

3 Lay the green felt over the wadding/batting towards the top, and the greenery pattern on top of the green felt. Pin through all layers.

4 Sew the outline of the greenery with dark green thread. Starting at the left side at the top of the lower inside leaf (which will rest on the flower pot), sew along the outline, turning sharply at the leaf points. Follow around the lower leaves and then the curves around the top, continuing down to the right and around the pointed leaves at the right and finishing at the top of the leaf that will be at the right of the flowerpot.

5 Change to light green thread. Make a second line just inside the dark green outline. Move to the bottom centre and sew a few stems up into the greenery and retrace to thicken the line. Sew some stems fanning out across the greenery, finishing back at the starting point.

6 Change to brown thread. Sew three seed heads. Starting at the bottom centre, sew up

Flowers and pot templates: enlarge to 200%

into the greenery, making the 'fork' by swinging out to the right; sew a few stitches at the top in a circular motion and back, then swing out to the left and sew the circular top as before. Go back to the centre and make two more stalks with heads in the same way as before, following back down the stem. Move to the right and make another seed head at a slight angle into the right side of the greenery and then move to the left to make a third seed head on the left side. Snip close to the edge of the bottom central leaves where they will sit over the flowerpot, leaving the remaining felt between them intact, as it will sit behind the flowerpot.

7 Change to brown thread. Cut the flowerpot shape from the brown felt. Place in position, sitting it under the leaves on either side and tucking the surplus from the centre underneath. Place the pattern on top and pin the centre and top of the flowerpot down through all the layers. Carefully fold and pin the lower leaves out of the way. Make the outline of the flowerpot, starting at the top left and sewing across the top, then turn sharply and follow all the way around the outline to the bottom; turn sharply at the bottom to travel up the left side, stopping to make the shading lines at the left side. Stop at the bottom of the rim, and sew across to the right and back again to the left, then continue up the left side of the rim making the shading lines before finishing at the starting point.

8 Unpin the folded leaves so that they fall back into place.

9 Change to black thread. Make the five flowers at the bottom. Cut circles about 1.5cm (½in) in diameter from the felt scraps and tack in place. To sew a flower shape, start in the centre, swing out slightly then back towards the edge, curving around to swing in the same way back to the centre. Repeat five or six times to complete the shape. Carefully trim away any excess. Place a tiny scrap of yellow felt over the centre of each flower and sew a circle shape. Trim away the excess yellow felt.

10 For the flower at the top, cut out a circle of white felt about 1.5cm (½in) in diameter and tack in place. To sew the petals, start at the centre top, swing out slightly then back towards the top, curving around to swing in the same way back to the centre. Repeat four times to complete the shape. Trim away any excess. Pin a small scrap of yellow felt over the top and sew around the outline. Trim away the excess.

11 Change to pink thread for the swirls. Working in any space, start at the outside and sew in a circular motion, curling inwards as you go.

12 Change to brown thread and repeat for more swirls.

13 Carefully cut around the whole shape leaving a margin.

14 Trim away excess wadding/batting and calico so that they sit just under the felt.

15 Place the work on the backing felt stretched in a hoop. Pin and stitch the outline. Using dark green thread, sew through all thicknesses around the outline of the greenery. Change to brown thread and follow the outline around the plant pot, including the lower rim.

16 Trim away any excess felt. Sew the brown swirls over the flowerpot.

17 Sew a brooch back onto the centre of the backing felt.

Beach Hut

Materials:

Tracing paper

Coloured felt, 9 x 8cm (3½ x 3¼in)

Scraps of felt or fabric for bunting

Coloured felt scraps for door and windows

Coloured felt for roof, 6 x 4cm (2¼ x 1½in)

Calico, 18 x 18cm (7 x 7in)

Wadding/batting, 9 x 8cm (3½ x 3¼in)

Backing felt, 18 x 18cm (7 x 7in)

Black thread

Brooch back

Tools:

16cm (6¼in) embroidery hoop

Sewing machine

Paper scissors

Fabric scissors

Embroidery scissors

Pins

Needle

Beach hut template: enlarge to 200%

Instructions:

1 Enlarge, trace and cut out the beach hut outline leaving a 1cm (½in) border. Trace and cut out the windows, roof and door shapes separately, again leaving a narrow border.

2 Stretch the calico on the hoop. Lay the wadding/batting centrally on top of the calico.

3 Lay the beach hut coloured felt on top of the wadding/batting and the paper pattern on top of the felt. Pin through all layers.

4 Sew the whole beach hut outline. Starting at the top of the roof, travel to the right down the outer roof line, turn in and down the right of the hut, turn sharply and sew along the bottom to the left corner, up the side then out and up to the top, following the apex shape all the way round. Turn sharply and continue down the right side of the roof line to the first 'plank' line across the roof space. Sew along the line to the left, turn sharply and follow along the outer roof line down to the next plank line. Sew across to the right, turn sharply and down to start the next line across. Continue in this way, sewing the plank lines right across the body of the beach hut until you reach the bottom.

5 Carefully tear away the paper pattern.

6 Lay the roof felt in position at the top of the beach hut. Lay the pattern on top of the felt, pin and tack through all layers. Sew around the roof line. Start at the top right of the apex shape, follow all the way around this shape then down the outer roof line, turn sharply, sew across and continue up to the top, around the apex point, then turn and sew around the left of the roof in the same way. Carefully remove the pattern and trim away excess roof felt.

7 Position the door felt in the centre, place the pattern on top and pin through all layers. Sew the door outline, turning sharply at the corners. Continue around the shape to turn and travel up, across and down the plank lines of the door, making the centre line thicker with an extra line of stitch. Sew the triangular outline of the door catch as shown. Carefully remove the pattern and trim away any excess felt from the door shape. Fill in the door catch shape.

8 Place the window felt in position with the pattern on top. Pin and tack in place. Sew the window outline, turning sharply at the corners. Continue along the outline to the start of the vertical cross line, travel down, then follow around to the horizontal line and sew across. Repeat for the second window. Carefully tear away the pattern. Trim away any excess felt from the window shapes.

9 Cut small triangles for the bunting, and place them in position. These are fiddly to sew, so pin and tack into place. Sew a row of stitch across the top of the bunting shapes, just catching them down from left to right.

10 Carefully cut around the whole beach hut outline leaving a margin.

11 Trim away excess wadding/batting and calico so that they sit just under the felt.

12 Place the work on the backing felt stretched in a hoop. Pin and stitch the outline. Start at the top and follow all the way around and back to the starting point, folding the end bunting flags out of the way as you go. Sew an extra row across the top of the bunting on top of the first to thicken.

13 Trim away any excess felt.

14 Sew a brooch back onto the centre of the backing felt.

Cupcake

Materials:

Tracing paper

'Cake' coloured felt, 9 x 8cm (3½ x 3¼in)

'Icing' coloured felt, 6 x 3cm (2¼ x 1¼in)

Scrap of red felt

Lilac felt, 6 x 5cm (2¼ x 2in)

Tulle or lace, 6 x 5cm (2¼ x 2in)

Calico, 18 x 18cm (7 x 7in)

Wadding/batting, 9 x 8cm (3½ x 3¼in)

Backing felt, 18 x 18cm (7 x 7in)

Black thread

Brooch back

Tools:

16cm (6¼in)
  embroidery hoop

Sewing machine

Paper scissors

Fabric scissors

Embroidery scissors

Pins

Needle

*Cupcake template:
enlarge to 200%*

Instructions:

1 Enlarge, trace and cut out the whole cake template leaving a 1cm (½in) border. Trace and cut the case, the icing and cherry shapes separately, again leaving a border.

2 Stretch the calico on the hoop. Lay the wadding/batting centrally on top of the calico.

3 Lay the cake coloured felt on top of the wadding/batting and the paper pattern on top of the felt. Pin through all layers.

4 Sew the whole cake outline. Starting at the top where the cherry will sit, follow the outline around the whole cake and back to the starting point. Carefully remove the pattern.

5 Place the lilac case felt in position, with the lace or tulle on top of the case felt and the pattern on top of the lace or tulle. Pin and tack into place.

6 Sew the outline of the case. Starting at the top right, sew down to the bottom right corner, turn sharply, follow along to the left corner, then turn sharply and continue up to the top left of the case. Turn sharply and follow the zigzag of the top of the case, finishing at the starting point. Turn around and follow the line to the first downward point of the pleats, follow the line down to the bottom, turn sharp left and along to the next line; follow up the line to the top at the bottom of the 'v'. Continue in this

way until all of the 'pleats' of the cake case are complete. Finish at the top left.

7 Carefully tear away the tracing paper pattern.

8 Carefully trim away the excess case felt and lace/tulle along the zigzag top.

9 Lay the 'icing' felt in position on the top of the cake, with the pattern on top of the icing felt, and pin through all layers.

10 Sew the icing shape, starting at the top where the cherry will sit, and follow round to the right; then follow the curves along the bottom line, continuing up the top left to the starting point.

11 Carefully remove the pattern. Trim away the excess 'icing' felt around the lower curves and where the cherry will sit.

12 Lay the red felt in place at the top of the cake, with the pattern on top, and pin and sew around the cherry. Carefully remove the pattern and trim away any excess cherry felt.

13 Carefully cut around the whole cake outline leaving a margin.

14 Trim away excess wadding/batting and calico so that they sit just under the felt.

15 Place the work on the backing felt stretched in a hoop. Pin and stitch the outline. Start at the top right of the cherry and follow all the way around and back to the starting point, continuing around the cherry to finish at the left.

16 Trim away any excess felt.

17 Sew a brooch back onto the centre of the backing felt.

Fairy

Materials:

Tracing paper

Skin-coloured felt, 10 x 9cm (4 x 3½in)
  plus extra scraps

Lilac felt, 7 x 5cm (2¾ x 2in)

Hair-coloured felt, 5 x 3cm (2 x 1¼in)

Scrap of plum-coloured felt

Organza, 3 x 5cm (1¼ x 2in)

Calico, 18 x 18cm (7 x 7in)

Wadding/batting, 10 x 9cm (4 x 3½in)

Backing felt, 18 x 18cm (7 x 7in)

Star-shaped bead or sequin

Small bead

Black thread

Brooch back

Tools:

16cm (6¼in)
  embroidery hoop

Sewing machine

Paper scissors

Fabric scissors

Embroidery scissors

Pins

Beading needle

Needle

*Fairy template:
enlarge to 200%*

Instructions:

1 This design requires several separate patterns. Enlarge, trace and cut out the outline of the whole fairy with just the wings marked, leaving a 1cm (½in) border. Trace the dress, legs and shoes together. Separately enlarge, trace and cut out the hair, the face, and the arm holding the wand, leaving a small border.

2 Stretch the calico on the hoop. Lay the wadding/batting centrally on top of the calico.

3 Lay the main skin-coloured felt on top of the wadding/batting and the pattern of the outline fairy with wings on top of the felt. Slide the organza under the pattern into the position of the wing area, so that it will get caught under the dress and hair. Pin and tack through all layers.

4 Sew the whole fairy and wings outline. Starting at the top left of the wing, travel to the tip of the left wing, turn and follow down to where the two wings meet, turn to sew down the line into the hair area and retrace back up until you reach the tip of the right wing. Turn sharply and sew down towards the dress. Continue to follow the outline all the way around the dress, legs, feet and lower arm until you reach the neck. Carefully remove the paper. Trim away excess organza from the outside of the wings.

5 Lay the dress/shoe felt in place, overlapping the bottom of the wings. Lay the dress, legs and shoes template on top of the felt, matching it to the stitched outline on the skin colour (paying particular attention to the position of the legs and feet). Pin and tack into place. Sew the dress outline starting at the top shoulder and following around the shape, turning corners sharply and following up and down the fold lines. Finish at the lower shoulder. Sew the outline of the shoes. Carefully remove the template and trim away excess dress and shoe felt to reveal the skin-coloured legs.

6 Place the hair felt in position and the hair template on top. Pin through all layers. Sew the hair outline starting at the left just under the face and follow the curves round to finish at the other side. Trim away excess felt around the curves. Do not trim away from the face area.

7 Lay a scrap of skin-coloured felt in position with the face pattern on top. Pin into place. Sew the outline of the face, then the curves of the eyes and mouth. Carefully remove the pattern and trim away excess felt from the face.

8 Lay a scrap of plum-coloured felt across the neckline. Sew three circles in a row. Sew over the circles again to thicken. Trim away excess necklace felt.

9 Lay a scrap of skin-coloured felt in position with the arm pattern on top. Starting at the top left, follow across to the hand, sew around the back of the hand and then up around the fingers; retrace the stitch lines of the fingers and sew along the lower part of the arm. Carefully tear away the pattern. Trim away any excess felt from the arm. Sew a short line horizontally across the lower arm for the armhole. To sew the wand stick, sew a line going up from the top of the hand into the wing and back down to thicken. Sew another line from the bottom edge of the hand into the dress section and back up to thicken.

10 Sew a star-shaped bead by hand at the top of the wand with a smaller bead sitting in the centre. Fasten on and off at the back of the work.

11 Carefully cut around the whole fairy outline leaving a narrow margin.

12 Trim away excess wadding/batting and calico so that they sit just under the felt.

13 Place the work on the backing felt stretched in a hoop. Pin and stitch the outline. Starting at the top wing, follow the outline sewing down and back up the line between the wings. Continue to follow all the way around the outline until you reach the starting point, sewing across and back at the top of the legs before continuing around the legs and again across and back at the top of the lower arm.

14 Trim away any excess felt.

15 Sew a brooch back onto the centre of the backing felt.

Stitching tips

Practising free machine stitching

Stretch some calico in a hoop. With a pencil draw some lines on the calico as a guide. Start with straight lines, then add zigzags, curves and loops. Place the prepared hoop under the sewing machine foot at the starting point. Drop the presser foot down, spool the thread to the top and stitch slowly along the lines.

Prepare another hoop. This time draw wherever you want to go directly with the machine. Try stopping and turning sharply. Try a circular movement; see how big and then how small you can go. Try wiggling a line. Try travelling backwards. Remember that the fabric will not travel on its own – you need to guide it firmly but steadily.

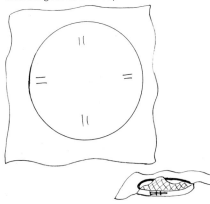

Stretching fabric in a hoop

Practising with different stitches

Stitching styles:

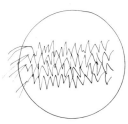

Furry style
Sew with a jerky movement, travelling across and back in zigzag lines to create the furry texture. Start at the top left, moving down with each row.

Sketchy style
Give a textured outline by randomly retracing back and forth as you travel.

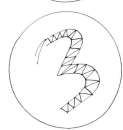

Zigzag style
Guide from left to right and back fairly evenly while travelling between two outlines.

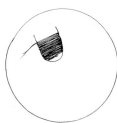

Filling style
Make the outer line first, then travel back and forth within the shape until filled.

Circular style
Guide the work by moving it in a circular motion as you travel.